CUSTOMS and COOKING FROM WALES

by Sian Llewellyn

Try some welsh cooking on
that Welsh husband of yours Helen,

Lots of Love

Barbara.

May. 1979.

ISBN 0 86005 0254 (Paper)
ISBN 0 86005 0246 (Cased)

CONTENTS

Use plain flour unless stated otherwise. Castor sugar is recommended for butter and sugar creamed mixtures.

A CUSTOMS CALENDAR FOR WALES

Old New Year's Day (12th January)
Event   New Year Celebrations
Place   Cwm Gwaun, Dyfed
Event   Church festival
Place   Llandysul, Dyfed

1st March
Event   St David's Day Celebrations
Place   Throughout Wales

Monday before Easter
Event   Easter Egg Clapping
Place   Anglesey

First Week of July
Event   International Musical Eisteddfod
Place   Llangollen, Clwyd

July 31st
Event   St Margaret's Fair
Place   Tenby, Dyfed

First Week of August
Event   Royal National Eisteddfod
Place   Different venue each year

During August
Event   The Ostreme Pageant
Place   Mumbles, Glamorgan

Saturday of the week including August 19
Event   Coracle race
Place· Cilgerran, Dyfed

The Christmas season
Event   Welsh carol singing
Place   Throughout Wales but especially the Tanad Valley, Clwyd and Powys
Event   Mari Lwyd mummers
Place   Pencoed and Abercrave, Glamorgan and elsewhere

CUSTOMS. . .

THE GREY MARE OR GREY MARY — MARI LWYD

The seasons have contributed to many Welsh customs. One which belongs traditionally to the Christmas season is known as the Mari Lwyd. Some believe that the ceremony comes from pagan rites welcoming the return of the sun after the winter solstice. In mediaeval times, the Mari Lwyd became associated with wassailing and it may have been adopted by the church to commemorate the purification of the Virgin Mary.

The Mari Lwyd consists of a horse's skull and jaws adorned with coloured ribbons, papers and streamers. This is carried on a pole or on a man's shoulders at the head of a procession. The man is draped in a white sheet and works the horse's lower jaw by means of a wooden handle. The Mari Lwyd is led from house to house in the district and at each the group ask permission to sing. The songs are composed of extempore verse which follows traditional rules — a number of verses are sung by those in the party and after each verse the occupants of each house reply with other verses. When this ritual is complete the Mari Lwyd is allowed into the house where the whole party is given food and drink, before moving on.

The custom has flourished throughout Wales and is still practised, especially in South Wales at Cardiff, Bridgend, Llangynwyd, Pencoed and Neath and also in Dyfed. An article in the 'South Wales Evening Post' of 29 December, 1973 suggests that in recent years the Mari Lwyd is thriving at both Christmas and the New Year. At Bryn Seion Chapel in the Swansea Valley the author writes, *'I met a group of villagers rehearsing songs and old Welsh carols in readiness for their Mari Lwyd celebration which takes place on New Year's Eve'.* He goes on to say

The Mari Lwyd tradition died out some 60 years ago in Abercrave. But last year Graham Pritchard, a civil servant who lives in the village, collected verses and songs from the oldest inhabitants who could still remember the tradition — and on New Year's Eve, 1972, the Abercrave Mari Llwyd went on its rounds again.

'Mari Lwyd could be translated in two ways', said Graham. 'In the Middle Ages mari was an acceptable Welsh word for mare, and it could also mean Maria or Mary.

It is obvious that at some time during the pre-Christmas times there was a cult of horse worship.

8

When christianity arrived in Wales the ceremony was retained and given a christianised meaning.

The people would go out any time between Christmas Eve and New Year's Eve — Nos Galan. In some parts of Pembrokshire it was practised on Christmas Eve, but in most parts of South Breconshire and north Glamorgan it was New Year's Eve.'.

The Abercrave Mari Lwyd, like every other true Mari Lwyd, is a Welsh custom which is performed entirely in Welsh.

In the same article the author refers to a Mari Lwyd which exists in the Mumbles district of Swansea. This is the only version of the tradition which is performed in English. He continues,

The Mumbles tradition is something of a mystery. In present form, it certainly isn't a true Mari Lwyd, but it may have had its roots in a long-lost Gower tradition. Over the last 100 years, though, it has been a unique hybrid of Welsh and English customs.   The Mumbles horse first appeared 101 years

ago this Christmas.

and then gives an interesting and amusing account of how the Mumbles custom originated. The 'horse' was a result of the tenacity of two Mumbles schoolboys

They had heard about the horses' heads that they used up the valleys, so they decided to get one too.

The horse who obliged was called Sharper. He used to pull a vegetable cart around Mumbles, and was buried at Barland, near Bishopston, when he died.

The boys dug him up, brought him back to Mumbles and buried him in lime. When the time came they cleaned him up in Mare's Pool, Tichbourne, used the bottoms of bottles for his eyes and wired his jaws together. They took him home where their mother helped to dress him up.

She didn't know how to dress him, but she made a hood for his head to pin rosettes on. He was covered with a sheet, with ribbons of every colour streaming down.

The boys were stuck for a song so they went to the curate of Oystermouth church and he composed a Horse's Head Song.

Armed with this song and another called the Mistletoe Bough, the boys were ready to go visiting.

In Sharper's heyday, the highlight of the Christmas season was Christmas Eve, when he would go up and down Mumbles Road, followed by half the village.

WASSAILING — GWASAEL

A custom often associated with the Mari Lwyd but which existed apart from it, was wassailing. Literally waes heil means 'be whole', and wassailing in its various forms was concerned with a primitive urge to induce fruitfulness or well-being. Health-drinking was associated with certain feast or holy-days, notably Christmas, the New Year, and Twelfth Night, that is feast days immediately preceding the New Year and the onset of spring. An example of the custom in the 1820's was described by Hugh Hughes in 1823 thus:—

'An old custom among the Welsh on Twelfth Night was the making of the wassail, namely, cakes and apples baked and set in rows on top of each other, with sugar between, in a kind of beautiful bowl which had been made for the purpose and which had twelve handles. Then warm beer, mixed with hot spices from India, was put in the wassail, and the friends sat around in a circle near the fire and passed the wassail bowl from hand to hand, each drinking in turn. Lastly the wassail (namely the cakes and apples after the beer covering them had been drunk) was shared among the whole company.

On Twelfth Night the wassail was taken to the house of a husband and wife who had recently married or a family which had moved from one house to another. Several lads and lasses from the neighbourhood would bring the wassail to the door of the said house and begin to sing outside the closed door.''

In passing it should be mentioned that many of the wassail bowls were made at the pottery near Ewenny, Bridgend. The early history of this pottery has still to be investigated but it is possible that it may have been associated in mediaeval times with Ewenny Priory (founded A.D. 1140). The pottery flourished in the late eighteenth and nineteenth centuries and made a number of the traditional bowls.

CAROL SERVICE — PLYGEINIAU

On the borders of Clwyd and Powys especially in the Tanad Valley it is traditional at Christmas time to hold a particular type of Christmas Carol service. This is known as the plygeiniau. It consists of male singers going from church to church during the season. At each church they render unaccompanied peformances of carols in Welsh.

HUNTING THE WREN — HELA'R DRYW

The widespread pagan custom of Hunting the Wren has persisted in Wales for centuries. The wren was supposed to embody the evils of winter and as such had to be trapped. In Pembrokeshire [Dyfed] the Hunting took place around the Twelfth Night after Christmas, and when the bird was captured it was placed in a carved be-ribboned 'wren house'. Four men then carried it round the town, singing of their prowess in capturing the bird, and confirming their willingness to sell their captive in order to buy beer.

NEW YEAR'S GIFTS — CALENNIG

A custom associated with the Christmas season was the collection of New Year gifts by children. This was known as Calennig. While the custom is, of course, widespread, in Glamorgan it took an interesting form. Fruit such as apples and oranges were decorated with sprigs of holly and with raisins and studded with grains of oats. Three wooden skewers were fixed in the fruit to form a tripod stand, and a fourth skewer formed a handle. These apples and oranges were carried by the children who sang traditional verses. The following are English examples of what they sang:—

'The snow lay on the ground, the star shone bright
When Christ our Lord was born on Christmas night.'

'Twas Mary, daughter of Holy Ann
That brought him to this world, our Lord made man'

'She laid him on the straw at Bethlehem,
The ass and oxen shared the room with them.'

NEW YEAR'S WATER — DŴR DYDD CALAN

At new year, at three or four o'clock in the morning, boys carrying a pitcher of cold spring, freshly drawn, water visited the homes of those in the area. This custom was traditional in South Wales, especially in Pembrokeshire[Dyfed]. The boys sprinkled water on the hands and faces of everyone they met. As well the boys carried twigs of box, myrtle, holly or other evergreen. Every room of every house they entered was sprinkled with water and if they could not enter, the doors were sprinkled. In Pendine, Carmarthenshire [Dyfed], a similar custom was practised on Old New Year's Day.

NEW YEAR'S DAY — DYDD CALAN

Before the Gregorian calendar was adopted by Britain in 1752, the New Year began on what is now 12th January. The people of the Gwaun Valley (Cwm Gwaun, Dyfed) still celebrate the old New Year's Day, Hen Galan, on that date. In the morning children go out to collect the traditional New Year gifts and in the evening there are parties to celebrate the beginning of the Year for the inhabitants.

In Tenby, Dyfed, it is traditional for children to sprinkle passers-by with fresh raindrops from twigs of box bush or holly. It is thought that the custom originated in pre-Christian days but by mediaeval times the practice was associated with Christianity and the Virgin Mary.

VALENTINES — FFOLANTAU

In the 17th century in Wales as in England a Valentine was a person not a letter or a card. In a ceremony it was traditional *'to draw lots which they term Valentines. The names of a select number of one sex are by an equal number of the other put into some vessel, and after that, everyone draws a name, which for the present is called their Valentine, and is also looked upon as a good omen of their being man and wife afterward'*. The custom is alluded to in Welsh manuscripts of this century by the Welsh phrase ei dynnu'n, falendein to draw him as a valentine.

A later form of the custom developed in Wales in the 18th century. At first it seems that the tokens were hand made. Marie Trevelyan asserts that it was the custom in Glamorgan to make true lovers' knots and to send them on Saint Valentine's Day. Young men during long winter nights spent some of their time tying lovers' knots — clymu cwlwm cariad. As time went on hand made letters replaced the love knots, a rhymed greeting being composed by a local poet or writer. In the 19th century, for example, in the Llandysul area of Cardiganshire, [Dyfed] young suitors used to visit Dewi Dyssul as he was called. He used to write amatory verses which were then written out by the young men and sent to their sweethearts.

In the early twentieth century ornate printed valentines became fashionable. One writer refers to the practice in South Wales of sending such valentines thus — *'The boys would be willing to pay about two shillings or half a crown for a valentine to send to their true loves. These were trimmed with a border of silk thread and ribbons, and flowers of all colours, and were packed in boxes. The girls used to keep these carefully and place them on the dresser after marrying and having a home of their own.'*

The transition from the hand-made to the factory-made valentine in Wales was gradual and in the late 19th and early 20th century it was usual for decorations still to be done by hand. By the late 1920's however, the more conventional machine-made valentines had replaced the earlier forms.

LOVE SPOONS — LLWYAU CARU

Between the 17th and 19th centuries, it was a widespread custom in Wales for young men to carve wooden spoons as love tokens for their sweethearts. The spoons were not meant to be used and many were intended to demonstrate how clever the man was with his hands — how skilfully he could carve.

The designs came to have a meaning of their own. Thus, two bowls carved from one handle meant 'we two are one'. Wheels and spades promised that the man would work hard for his intended bride and miniature houses that they would make a home together. The handles were very ornate and hearts were frequent motifs, one signified 'my heart is yours' and two suggested that the feelings for one another were mutual. The spoon itself was symbolical of the fact that the suitor would provide for his loved one. Those with ships and anchors were probably carved by sailors, the ship implying that the suitor had found a harbour for his heart and the anchor suggested that the sailor wished to stay with his love.

The imagery of marriage and childhood were frequent themes. Many spoons had long handles with cavities or lanterns in which spheres of wood ran freely up and down but remained captured by the frame of the spoon. This meant that the man was trapped by his love for his sweetheart and could not be freed until she returned his affection. Bows and knots on the spoon showed that the suitor was anxious to tie the marriage knot. Some spoons had two large bowls and a middle miniature one which spoke touchingly of 'it', the son or daughter who, it was hoped, would bless the union.

Although the practice of giving love spoons had almost stopped by the end of the 19th century, the interest in them has revived today. Many have a new and wider significance and some spoons are now carved as commemorative ornaments of major events, places and people. The Welsh Craft Industry also provides replicas of the 'old' spoons and miniature silver spoons for those who want a lasting memento of their visit to Wales.

SAINT DAVID'S DAY — DYDD GŴYL DDEWI

On 1st March of every year the people of Wales celebrate Saint David's Day. Throughout the principality the patron saint is remembered in verse and song and Welshmen and those with strong connections with this country wear a daffodil or leek, traditional emblems of Wales.

The origin of Saint David's Day lies in the life and work of our patron saint. We do not know when Saint David was born but it is thought that he lived during the second half of the fifth century and the first half of the sixth century. His mother was a young Welsh girl named Non and his father Sant, son of King Ceredig. The cottage where they lived overlooked the Bay of Non in Pembrokeshire.

The young boy lived his early life at Hen Fynyw and there he grew up into manhood. He had a strong sense of purpose and studied for the priesthood. Later, he studied under the scribe Paulinus, himself a disciple of Saint Germanus. When Paulinus became blind it is said that David touched and blessed his eyes and his master's sight was restored.

Soon after this, David felt called to missionary work. He founded monasteries at such places as Leominster, Glastonbury, Repton, and Llangyfelach.

Most of the stories about Saint David revolve around the place where he founded one of the twelve monasteries he started. This was about A.D. 530 at a place called Glyn Rhosyn the vale of roses, in Pembrokeshire [Dyfed]. It is on this site that the small cathedral city of Saint David's stands today. When David first came to Glyn Rhosyn the whole area was terrorised by a local chief named Boia and his wife. Ignoring their insults and plots David founded the monastery. Boia's wife urged him to drive out the monks and when he wavered she sent her maid-servants naked to the monastery in order to tempt the monks to break their vows of chastity. But David's example was followed by the other monks and they sent the girls away.

Saint David imposed a very austere life on the monastery — the monks worked throughout the day and prayed half the night; they shared the tools they used and ate simple meals of bread, herbs and water. Saint David preached obedience and cared for the sick, needy, orphans and widows. The Saint became famous for his ascetism and hard discipline. Saint David drank only water (Dewi Ddyfawr — David the Water-Drinker) and was the first Welshman who pledged himself to teetotalism. All work was carried on in religious silence and property belonged to all — any monk who accidently said *'my book'* or *'my cup'* had to expiate the offence with a severe penance.

Saint David eventually became one of the most important leaders in the Celtic Church and disciples flocked to him. Like many saints whose exploits were recorded centuries after their deaths, Saint David has been credited with many miracles. For example, legend says there was no water near his monastery until he prayed. Then, a mature spring appeared at his feet. Again, he is said to have been responsible for the well at Ffynnon Feddyg near Aberayron, Cardiganshire [Dyfed]. At this water source the blind regained their sight and the lame were made to walk again.

Later in his life David journeyed abroad to Jerusalem and there he was made a bishop by the Patriarch. When he returned home a meeting of the Celtic Church was held at a Synod in Llanddewibrefi in Cardiganshire (A.D. 519). The assembled bishops found it difficult to make themselves heard above the noise of the vast throng. Saint David had no trouble at all for he is said to have made the ground on which he stood into a hill and from there his voice could be heard by all. A church called Llanddewibrefi was dedicated to him and still stands on top of the reputedly miraculous hill.

Saint David probably died on 1 March, 589 and it is said that a host of singing angels bore him to heaven. Since that day March 1st has been celebrated as the National Day of Wales.

The leek is one of the national emblems of Wales. It is associated with Saint David who was reputed to have *fed upon the leeks* that *he gathered in the fields.* At the battle of Heathfield in A.D. 633 Welshmen wore leeks when fighting against the Saxon invaders. In mediaeval times we know that Welshmen wore leeks at the battle of Crécy and, in Tudor times, presents of leeks were given to the Royal family by soldiers coming from Wales. Nowadays, the leek is worn on Saint David's Day and sported by Welshmen at International Rugby Matches.

The daffodil is the other national emblem of Wales. It probably owes its popularity to the fact that in Welsh it is known as cenhinen pedr (Peter's Leek) or cenhinen fawrth (March Leek). People believed that because of its name it was the national emblem and old customs die hard. Its beauty meant that once used the daffodil came to stay.

THE LIGHTED CANDLE — Y GANNWYLL OLEUEDIG

In earlier times the gradual change from winter to spring was highlighted by the feast of Candlemas (2nd February). Gwyl Fair Y Canhwyllau — Mary's Festival of Candles originated before the 16th century and was derived from the Catholic tradition of blessing the candles and distributing them to the people who would then take part in a solemn candle-bearing procession.

The tradition eventually lost its religious significance but candles were still lit in many areas of Wales to herald the advent of spring. Marie Trevelyan, for example, mentions in her book 'Folk-Lore and Folk-Stories of Wales' that on Candlemas Day it was the custom *'many years ago for people to light two candles, and place them on a table or high bench. Then each member of the family would in turn sit down on a chair between the candles. They each took a drink out of a horn goblet or beaker, and afterwards threw the vessel backwards over his head. If it fell in an upright position 'it was believed that 'the person who threw it would live to reach a very old age; if it fell bottom upwards, the person would die early in life.'*

SAINT BRYNACH'S CROSS — CROES SANT BRYNACH

There are numerous early Christian monuments and crosses in Wales. One of the finest Celtic crosses in Wales can be seen in the churchyard at Nevern, Pembrokeshire. (Dyfed). Known as Saint Brynach's Cross it dates from the 10th or 11th century. According to local tradition, the first cuckoo to be heard each year in Pembrokeshire perches on the top of the cross and sings on St. Brynach's Day (7th April).

EASTER EGG CLAPPING — CLAPIO AM WY PASG

At Easter time, eggs, the emblem of fertility, are particularly significant. In many parts of North Wales *the custom of clapping for eggs* was traditional on the Monday before Easter. The children of the district using small wooden clappers, not much larger than castanets and making approximately the same sound, chanted the words *Clap, clap, ask for an egg for little boys on the parish.* Often the chanting was omitted, the noise of the clappers being enough to indicate what they were about. In this way the children could collect as many as fifty eggs. When eggs were not available in some districts they might be given pennies.

THE HOLY GRAIL — Y GREAL SANCTAIDD

Between the courses of the rivers Ystwyth and Rheidol in Dyfed is the estate of Nanteos. The large house in its own grounds is the resting place for a wooden cup claimed to be the Holy Grail, the cup used at the Last Supper. The cup is reputed to have supernatural healing and curative powers and is now so aged that it is practically eaten away. It is guarded jealously by the present owner of Nanteos.

WELSH WELLS — FFYNHONNAU CYMRU

The coins at the bottom of the well each carried a wish, a dream, whispered secretly to the air. Some still gleam but others are half covered by mud.

There are wells all over the Principality and the sick and crippled have sought relief at Healing or Holy Wells from pre-Christian times.

The most famous of Welsh wells is at Holywell, Clwyd. Legend recalls that in the 7th century a tribal chief named Caradoc cut off the head of saint Winifred for refusing his amorous advances. Water sprang from the ground where her head fell. Her uncle, Saint Beuno is said to have restored the head to her body and she became Abbess of Gwytherin in Denbighshire [Clwyd]. Nicknamed 'Queen of the Wells', the waters were said to have miraculous healing properties especially for nervous disorders. By the 16th century it had such a reputation that it escaped the destruction wrought on many of such shrines during Henry VIII's dissolution of the monasteries. All manner of ailments were treated including chronic ill-health and sterility. Each morning, even today, there is a service for the sick at the church built there.

At the ruins of Carreg Cenan Castle, four miles from Llandeilo, Dyfed, there is a narrow, underground tunnel. One hundred and fifty feet long it leads to a famous wishing well. Here, visitors once threw corks and pins into the water and made wishes as they did so. The water was reputed to be able to heal eye and ear complaints and many people came to bathe.

At Glasfryn, Gwynedd, a story is told about a well house. One day, according to legend, a woman called Grace left the door open after she had drawn water. Immediately, the water began to flow out, flooded her house and turned her into a graceful swan. A lake now stands at the spot.

On Llanddwyn Island, Anglesey, there is a well named after a Celtic Saint, Dwynwen. Distressed lovers used to pray there for success in their love life or for forgetfulness. At Mynydd Penrhys, Glamorgan, there was a well where in the 16th century people went to have their 'dead returned to life'. There was a well on the east bank of the river Taff in Glamorgan from Roman times and as late as the

19th century, it was used for healing rheumatism, lameness and other chronic complaints.

A well of a different kind existed at Llaneilian — yn — Rhos, Clwyd. This village, situated near Colwyn Bay, had a famous cursing well. Anyone who wanted to damn an enemy would pay the custodian of the well a fee to write his enemy's name on a piece of paper. This was then wrapped around a pebble and dropped into the water. The curse was believed to last as long as the paper remained immersed and some victims went as far as to pay the custodian to remove their names. In 1831 one custodian was sentenced to six months' hard labour for accepting money under false pretences. The well was covered over in 1929 but its site can still be seen today.

At one well in North Wales people had to bathe in the waters at sunset, pay fourpence and spend the night in the chapel nearby. At another well at Llandeilo, Dyfed, a peculiar custom is recorded. People who suffered from respiratory diseases such as whooping cough or consumption used to drink water from St Teilo's Well. For a cure to be assured, the water had to be drunk from St. Teilo's skull, which had to be handed to the sufferer by the heir of a Llandeilo farm. The custom, and the skull, disappeared in 1927.

KING ARTHUR'S STONE — MAEN CETI ARTHUR
[Carreg Y Brenin Arthur]

At midnight when the moon was full, a young girl crept quietly from her bed and stole across the Common. The grass was wet beneath her feet and the tiny, busy creatures of the night scurried away from her footsteps. The Common seemed much bigger than in daytime and suddenly the girl started to run and fear ran behind her with silent footsteps.

At last she reached the stone and placed the honey-cake on top of it. Then she knelt on her hands and knees and crawled around the stone.

King Arthur's stone stands at the top of Cefn Bryn Common near Reynoldston. It is traditionally thought to be the 'pebble' which King Arthur removed from his boot when he was on the way to the Battle of Camlann in A.D. 539. He is said to have taken off his boot and thrown the stone over his shoulder and it landed seven miles away at this spot.

Until the end of the 19th century, local girls would place a honey-cake soaked in milk on the stone. Then, they would crawl around the stone three times on their hands and knees. They believed that, if their lovers were true, they would, after this ceremony, come and join them.

SAINT BEUNO'S CHEST — CIST
SANT BEUNO

An old strong-box curiosity exists in the 15th century church of St Beuno, Clynnog Fawr, Caernarvanshire. Made from a single piece of oak it is associated with an ancient custom. This was that calves born with mis-shapen ears were sold every year in the churchyard and the proceeds from their sales would be donated to the church through the use of St Beuno's Chest.

MERLIN'S GRAVE — BEDD MYRDDIN

For many hundreds of years Bardsey Island, two miles off the mainland of Gwynedd, was an important place for pilgrims. According to tradition thousands of monks and clergymen are buried there. Also the wizard Merlin is reputed to have a cave on the island. Surrounded by his treasures he will, according to tradition, awaken from his sleep when King Arthur returns from the dead.

MERLIN'S TREE — COEDEN MYRDDIN

In the South Wales town of Carmarthen, Dyfed, there stands a famous oak tree carefully preserved by the town's dignitaries. This is, according to tradition, Merlin's tree. A prophecy is connected with the tree which goes like this,

> When Merlin's tree shall tumble down,
> Then shall fall Carmarthen town.

Some people believe that Merlin is still alive and held prisoner in a cave at Bryn Myrddin, Merlin's Hill, about two miles east of Carmarthen. He is kept there in bonds of enchantment by his beloved Vivien. His mistake was, apparently, to have allowed this women to know his secret spells and some say they can hear the great magician's groans as he laments his folly.

ST MARGARET'S FAIR, TENBY — FFAIR
Y SANTES MERERID, DINBYCH Y PYSGOD

Tenby, Pembrokeshire, has had a long and chequered history. It probably started as a horse settlement and by the 9th century was a Welsh stronghold. It guards its ancient traditions, and every year since mediaeval times it holds a fair. The fair is held on 31st July and is opened by the mayor and the council walking in procession round the town walls.

THE SEASONAL FAIRS OF MACHYNLLETH — FFEIRIAU
TYMHOROL MACHYNLLETH

A picturesque tradition in Machynlleth, Powys is the continuation of the centuries — old seasonal fairs, in Maen Gwyn Street. At one time labourers offered their services to farmers by sporting a wheat-ear in their caps — these were the famous hiring fairs which no longer exist. What does remain is the huckster fairs. Travelling traders, gipsies amongst them offer bargains in pots and pans, jewels and jumpers, sweets and sweaters by way of Dutch auction. This is a system of putting a price on a set of goods and adding an additional item or items until someone agrees to buy. The repetition *'Un etto! Un etto!'* *('and another! and another!') is a familiar cry to those who gather around and even non-Welsh speakers have learnt the phrase.*

THE ANCIENT CHARTER OF LAUGHARNE — SIARTER
HYNAFOL TALACHARN

The ancient borough of Laugharne in Carmarthenshire is well known as the home of Dylan Thomas, one of Wales finest poets. It is not so well known that this small town is also a place of ancient traditions. Thus, for example, it still follows the provisions of the original charter granted to the borough by Sir Guy de Brian in 1307.

Laugharne still has a Portreeve who wears a chain of golden cockleshells around his neck, and he has halberdiers, mattockmen, flagbearers and guides attending him. The Corporation toasts the founder of the borough at the annual Portreeve's banquet.

SAINT DOGMAEL'S BLESSING — BENDITH
LLANDUDOCH

A tradition which died hard was the blessing ceremony at Saint Dogmael's (Llandudoch) Dyfed. At Carreg y Fendith the stone of blessing, beside the River Teifi, monks in the middle ages blessed the fish and prayed for a good harvest during the ensuing fishing season.

The custom was revived in 1965 but lapsed when a poor season followed.

CORACLE RACING — RASYS CORYGLAU

The coracle is an ancient British round-boat originally said to have been made of a slender frame of wood covered with skins. It was described thus in 1775:- *It is in shape oval, near three feet broad, and four feet long; a small keel runs from the head to the stern; a few ribs placed across the keel, and a ring of pliable wood around the lip. The whole is covered with the rough hide of an ox or a horse; the seat is in the middle; it carries but one person, or, if a second goes into it to be wafted over a river, he stands behind the rower, leaning on his shoulders.*

Nowadays, there are two types of coracles. Both are made of intertwined laths of willow and hazel and both are extremely light in weight. They are confined in use today to the rivers Teifi and Tywi in West Wales and different conditions on these rivers mean that the craft are different in appearance. Those used in the Teifi are designed to face rapid movement in the waters with a slender waist amidships. The Tywi coracle on the other hand is almost oval in shape and suits the peaceful waters of that river.

At Gilgerran, Dyfed, an annual coracle week is held in mid-August (14th-20th August approximately). The week includes exhibitions of the 5½ feet long craft, manoeuvering the boats with their single paddles made of ash, and invitation and impromptu races. Demonstrations of how these craft weighing 30-34 lbs each are carried and how fishermen work in pairs with a net suspended between two coracles are given.

KNAPPAN, QUOITS, HORSE AND CAR RACING — CNAPAN, COETENAU, RASYS CEFFYLAU A CHEIR

Besides the racing of coracles Wales has had a number of sports and games which were traditional. The Knappan is one of these. In this game, played at Newport, Pembrokeshire [Dyfed], a leather ball sewn and stuffed was pursued with sticks by horsemen — a sort of polo. At Llansawel, Carmarthenshire, there is a tradition of quoit playing, the quoits being made from the flat stones of the river bed. An annual football match was played between Llandysul and its neighbour Llanwenog the teams being made up of all inhabitants of each place, and the goals the porches of the churches of the respective places.

Sulkies, specially light two wheeled carriages are a feature of the races at Penybont, Radnorshire. Reminiscent of trotting horses in the U.S.A., these races still take place in Penybont today.

A modern sport has taken place since the 20's on the Pendine sands. Pendine has over five miles of sand that is so firm that cars can be driven on to the beach. The flat sand became the venue for famous

races and would-be record breakers. In such a tradition Parry Thomas, the Welsh ace, attempted to break the world record there but was killed. His car was buried in the sand dunes but has now been exhumed and remains a lasting memorial to Thomas and a tribute to an important era in British car development.

THE CAERWYS TRADITION — TRADDODIAD
CAERWYS

The small town of Caerwys, Clwyd, has had a tradition of music and poetry ever since the 12th century. Not only was it important in establishing a national eisteddfod but it also nurtured a band of wandering harpists, living by their skills and going from place to place throughout the year. The Tudors recognised the role of Caerwys in Welsh traditions and granted a commission to twenty gentlemen of North Wales to summon a meeting of wandering minstrels there. Wandering harpists continued from these times until the 19th century.

Caerwys was important, too, for its fairs. The drovers brought their cattle to these weekly events and passed through the town on the great cattle-trek to England. The cattle were shod in Caerwys ready for the great trek.

THE WHITE STICK — Y FFON WEN

The white stick was a token sent by a young lady to her rejected suitor or vice versa. It was a hazel twig of varying thickness freshly peeled of its bark. It was sent anonymously to a jilted lover on or near the wedding day of the former lover. In some parts of Wales a piece of ginger was used instead.

THE WOODEN HORSE — Y CEFFYL PREN

This custom existed in various parts of Wales and was connected with the sanctity of the marriage vows and familiar patterns in family life. Divorce was anathema to country folk and thus they adopted their own forms of corrective devices to punish those outside the accepted norm. In Carmarthen and south-west Wales a practice existed similar to the Skimmington ride described by Thomas Hardy in 'The Mayor of Casterbridge.' In west-Wales a person or his effigy was carried on a wooden pole so as to make him ridiculous in the community. This was often done when a wife took over command of the household and dominated her husband.

Other practices existed for different 'offences.' Thus, if a man or woman was faithless to their marriage vows the mob were likely to seize the offending pair and fasten them back to back on a wooden horse. They would then parade them throughout the district proclaiming their wrong-doing and pelting them with rotten fruit and bad eggs.

Similar variations of the same custom existed elsewhere. Thus, the ceffyl pren was used to punish those who had given evidence in unpopular legal cases. Other forms of the custom were extant, such as the practice of tying straw round the gate of a married couple's house when the husband had been beating his wife, *so that he might beat the straw instead of his wife'* (in Gwent) or burning in effigy as in Oswestry.

THE BIDDING — Y GALW

Parry Jones in his 'Welsh Country Upbringing' tells us about the custom of the bidding. Before a wedding took place guests were invited to the ceremony and to the reception. This was done either by sending a written request — a *'bidding letter'* — for people to attend or appointing a bidder to call at the homes of friends and acquaintances. Bradley in his 'Highways and Byways in South Wales' records such a bidding and M. Curtis in 'Antiquities of Laugharne' tells us about the bidder in that village in the 1840's. Called John Williams, 'He would be dressed in a white apron; a white ribbon was tied in the button-hole of his coat, and the bidder's staff in his hand with which he knocked at the doors. No one now remembers any ribbons at the end of it. A bag was swung at his back, in which he put the bread and cheese the people at the farmhouses gave the bidder. His Rammas (the form in which the invitation rhymes were framed) is described as most amusing . . . . It is as follows:-

'I was desired to call here as a messenger and a bidder. David J. and Anne W. in this parish of Laugharne, the hundred of Derllys, Co. Carmarthen, encouraged by their friends to make a bidding on Tuesday next; the two young people made their residence in Gosport, No 11, thence to St Michael's church to be married. The two young people return back to the young woman's father and mother's house to dinner. They shall have good beef and cabbage, mutton and turnips, pork and potatoes, roast goose or gant, perhaps both if they are in season, a quart of drink for fourpence, a cake for a penny, clean chairs to sit down upon, clean pipes and tobacco, and attendance of the best; a good song, but if no one will sing, then I'll sing as well as I can; and if no one will attend, I'll attend as well as I can. As a usual custom with us, in Laugharne, is to hold a 'sending gloves' before the wedding, if you'll please to come, or send a waggon or a cart, a horse and a colt, a heifer, a cow and a calf, or an ox and a half, or pigs, cocks, hens, geese, goslings, ducks, turkeys, a saddle and bridle, or a child's cradle, or what the house can afford. A great many can help one, but one cannot help a great many, or send a waggon full of potatoes, a cartload of turnips, a hundred or two of cheeses, a cask of butter, a sack of flour, a winchester of barley, or what you please, for anything will be acceptable; jugs, basins, saucepans, pots and pans, or what you can; throw in £5 if you like; gridirons, frying-pans, tea-kettles, plates and dishes,

30

a lootch (wooden spoon) and dish, spoons, knives and forks, pepper boxes, salt cellars, mustard pots, or even a penny whistle or a child's cradle. Ladies and gentleman, I was also desired to ask that all payments due to the young woman's parents and relations and the same due to the young man's . . . . be returned to the young people on the same day. So no more at present. If you please to order your butler, or underservant, to give a quart of drink to the bidder.' Variations of this speech occurred in various parts of South Wales and West Wales where the 'bidding' occurred most. In some parts of West Wales he would tell a story as part of the 'bidding'.

With the advent of the penny post the bidder was replaced by a bidding letter which followed a set pattern. An example of a bidding letter is as follows.

August, 25, 1798

Having lately entered the Matrimonial State, we are encouraged by our friends to make a Bidding on the occasion, on Thursday the 13th Day of September next, at the Dwelling House of Daniel Thomas (the young Woman's Father) called Iscoed Mill, in the Parish of St. Ishmael, at which place we humbly solicit the Favor of your good company; and whatever Donation you may then be disposed to bestow on us, will be gratefully received, and cheerfully repaid, whenever demanded on the like Occasion, by

Your most obliged humble servants,
Ebenezer Jones
Mary Jones.

An essential task for the bidder was to keep accurate accounts of moneys and gifts received. The young couple looked on the presents as debts that they would have to repay in kind later. As much as fifty pounds — a considerable sum in those days — would be collected at biddings and this enabled the pair to get married and set up home.

This custom had died out by the early twentieth century (but see the reference to a similar custom in the section on The Ostreme Pageant).

THE HYDDGEN STORY — CHWEDL HYDDGEN

Not long ago a circle of white stones could be seen at a spot on the Hyddgen, (The Hyddgen is a large area of lake and sheeplands in Dyfed). Now scattered by a new Forestry Commission road the white stones were originally designed to record a story.

The legend concerns an ageing shepherd and his wife who lived in this area. One day coming home on horseback, the shepherd was overtaken by blinding snow at the top of Bwlch Hyddgen. A little further on he fell exhausted from the saddle and the horse cantered on. Awakened by the riderless mount the wife left their home, and walked almost a mile until she reached her unconscious husband. She managed to drag him back alone to their cottage but by the time she had got him home he had died. She too died not long after. The tradition is that to this day a light comes from their cottage at Hyddgen and then moves to the place where the man fell from his horse and was found by his wife.

THE ABRACADABRA CHARM — SWYN ABRACADABRA

At a small village in Powys known as Casgob there was unearthed earlier this century a charm which is evidence of an early faith in Wales. Nicknamed the Abracadabra Charm there is a message written on it which contains a peculiar admixture of pagan belief in evil spirits and Christianity:-

'In the name of the Father, Son and of the Holy Ghost, Amen XXX and in the name of the Lord Jesus Christ who will deliver Elizabeth Lloyd from all witchcraft and from all evil sprites by the same power as he did cause the blind to see the lame to walke the dum to talke. Pater pater pater noster noster noster ave ave ave Maria in secula seculorum X on X Adonay X Tetragrammaton X Amen and in the name of the Holy Trinnity and of Hubert . . . . Grant that this holy charm Abracadabra may cure thy survent Elizabeth Lloyd from all evil sprites and all their desises. Amen XXX by Jah Jah Jah.'

A MERRY EVENING — NOSON LAWEN

The custom of the noson lawen dates back to the 17th century. It owes its origin to the need for community life and neighbourliness of the small rural communities in Wales at that time. The long summer days were work-days when the harvests were gathered in and the many and varied tasks of the farms were all important. In winter, however, with the coming of shorter days the evenings were long and some amusement had to be found.

Gatherings were held in the large kitchens of the farms or in barns. Plenty of food was provided and talk led to poetry, song and dance. Penillion were sung to the music of harp and crwth. Sometimes competitions took place when singers had to compose verses to the tunes being played, and in the metre and subject established by the first singer.

Stories were told and these included folk tales and ghost stories as well as the gossip of the farms and villages. The youngsters danced in groups and reels and jigs were popular. Sometimes they danced together in Clog, Poker or Trencher dances. Refreshments included home-made ale and the entertainment often went on until the early hours of the morning.

THE EISTEDDFOD — YR EISTEDDFOD

The Eisteddfod is perhaps the best known of Welsh customs and institutions. It has its origins in mediaeval times and now, as then, is a series of contests by poets, writers and musicians to establish the best amongst them. The earliest recorded contest of poets and musicians was at Cardigan Castle in 1176 and chair prizes were awarded to the winners. Unfortunately, there is no record of similar contests in the 13th and 14th centuries but we do have records of those held in the 15th and 16th centuries.

At Caerwys in 1568 an eisteddfod was held and its importance is highlighted by the prizes that were awarded — a miniature silver chair to the winning poet, a little silver 'crwth' to the winning fiddler, a silver tongue to the finest singer, and a small silver harp to the best harpist. This harp, only six inches long, is still in existence today.

At first, the contests were restricted to professional bards who were paid by the local nobility. This was a good idea while the local gentry were Welsh but as time went on English spread and the Welsh arts declined. A revival took place during the year of the French Revolution, however, under the auspices of Thomas Jones of Corwen. In 1789 he organised an eisteddfod at Corwen, Clwyd, to which, for the first time, the public were admitted. The eisteddfod was very successful and encouraged others to support regional eisteddfodau. In turn this led to an awakening of real interest in Welsh literature, music and the arts.

It is from such origins that the national Eisteddfod, held annually during August, comes. Many thousands of people congregate and the competitions have extended to Art, Crafts as well as Music and Literature. The competitions include crafts associated with industry, ambulance work, choral and orchestral competitions, brass band contests, competitions in composing poetry and prose, drama (acting and writing) and local crafts. The whole of the proceedings are conducted in Welsh and the National visits North and South Wales in alternate years.

Nowadays, a National Eisteddfod Council controls the event and includes members of the

Gorsedd. The aim of the Gorsedd is to *'ensure the co-operation of bards, men of letters, musicians and the patrons of the fine arts, in order to enrich bardism, literature, music and art in Wales.'* It also controls the rites and customs of the bards and is governed by the Archdruid who is elected from among the Druids for three years.

Much of the ceremonial associated with the National Eisteddfod comes from the Gorsedd. For example, they meet publicly to proclaim the following year's Eisteddfod at least a year and a day in advance. Robed in green, blue and white with the high officers wearing their symbolic regalia, the Gorsedd assembles within a circle of massive stones arranged on a traditional plan. Then 'in the face of the sun — the eye of light' the protection of God is invoked in the Gorsedd prayer. During the Eisteddfod, too, the Gorsedd undertakes meetings, and processions and ceremonies like 'crowning' the poet presenting the best Pryddest (an ode in free metres) and 'chairing' the poet presenting the winning Awdl (poem composed of strict, traditional, alliterative verse in Welsh).

During the second week of July an International Musical Eisteddfod takes place at Llangollen, Clwyd. The first 'International' was held from 11th to 15th June, 1946 and people wondered whether any international competitors would arrive to justify the title. But come they did; forty overseas groups, representing fourteen nations. The International Eisteddfod has been held every year since. Competitors today come from over thirty countries to take part in choral and folk singing, and dancing. Nowadays, the event is held during the second week of July and the small town then becomes a kaleidescope of colour and cacophony of sounds. The artists, dressed in their colourful national costumes sing and dance in the parks and open places. The main events take place in a huge marquee set up in the valley between the mountains and up to 100,000 people come to listen and to watch.

THE OSTREME PAGEANT — Y PASIANT OSTREME

Ancient tradition meets with modern social consciousness in the annual Ostreme Pageant which takes place in August in Mumbles near Swansea, Glamorgan. The name Ostreme was adopted for the festival and pageant as it was the name given to Oystermouth by the Romans, and in earlier days Mumbles was the centre of a thriving oyster industry.

The first Ostreme celebrated time-honoured Welsh customs. Thus, on Wednesday 8th August, 1973, a traditional wedding was held in the British Legion Hall as part of the Pageant. The whole village joined in the celebrations and instead of sending out invitations the bridal couple sent the wedding beader to the homes of their friends. He knocked at the door of each house with a staff decorated with ribbons and invited the guests to *have good meat and good music and dancing as for as lieth in my power.'*

One can imagine the great excitement created by such events in earlier times. Those invited to a wedding whether relatives or friends used to take currant loaves as gifts to the wedding — house the day before. These were called 'present' and were sliced and sold at supper time to the young men, who then gave them secretly to the ladies they admired. At the end of the supper the girl with the greatest number of slices of 'present' was regarded as the most eligible and likely to be married next time there was a wedding.

On the wedding-day the guests followed the bride and a fiddler to go to church. Like the beader's staff, the violin of this musician would be streamed with ribbon. After the service the brides — for both groom and bride were called this, went with their relatives and friends to the local inn to take refreshment. A full dinner would be served at the wedding-house where the main celebrations took place. The way there was sometimes barred by a rope stretched across the road, and even a gunshot or two! This 'hold-up' resulted in the payment of a small amount of money as a ransom, and this custom was called 'chaining the brides'. Dinner was then served at the wedding-house, with mutton pies baked in shallow tins the popular food, called 'tinmeat'. The beader would solicit what monetary gifts he could from the guests — and record the amount in his book. Gifts from married couples were straight-forward presents, but the gifts of unmarried people were the 'heavings' which were acknowledged as being due back as presents when the giver married.

Another supper would be held on the wedding-night, this time open to all who paid the few shillings' fee, and tin-meat again appeared. The fiddler provided the music for a dance, and as the evening wore on girls were obliged to choose which of their admirers they would have for an escort. Sometimes this led to fighting among the jealous rivals turned down by popular girls. 'Pawling' was the name given this choosing of suitors.

This, a variation of the bidding ceremony described earlier, is typical of the traditional Welsh ceremonies recalled at Ostreme.

Part of the 1973 celebrations paid tribute to famous Welshmen. Oystermouth Castle was the backcloth to a historical Pageant which included Major Grenfell who took command of the marines aboard the 'Victoria' while Dylan Thomas, who spent much of his time in the Mumbles and its taverns, was remembered in the Festival's production of 'Under Milk Wood'.

WELSH COSTUME — Y WISG CYMRAEG

The origin of 'Welsh National Costume' is obscure. Descriptions in literature, the testimony of wills, and inventories where garments are listed, household accounts, family letters and portraits as well as survivals of the actual clothes from the late 16th century, suggest that there was no such costume for well-to-do people.

Even for the less well to do — and here we have the additional evidence of drawings and water-colours down to the eighteenth century — there is nothing specifically or characteristically Welsh in the garments described. The roots of Welsh National Costume can first be found in the dress of the late 17th and early 18th centuries. This costume, worn over a wide area, had the open fronted gown with a shirt hitched back showing the petticoat. Then there was the long apron protecting the front of the petticoat and the wide collar which covered the low neck line in the same way that the neckerchiefs and small shawls of the Welsh costume did later. It must be admitted, however, that for these garments as well as the tall beaver hat worn by many from the 17th century, there was nothing exclusively Welsh or English for that matter, about them. *'It is plain that the answer to the question about this dress being a Welsh national one is a decided negative. It was worn by part of the community only, and garments of a similar kind and cut, although often of different materials, were worn by some English country women also'* *

In the 18th century it is clear, for example, that the hats worn by the women were made of felt and very similar to the men's. They were low crowned and unlike the tall hats which became so familiar later. Samuel Rush Meyrick's 'History of Cardiganshire (1808) asserts that throughout Wales women wore the same hats, shoes and buckles as the men. Moreover, there were few if any regional differences in the clothes worn. Many writers keen to emphasize the Welshness of Wales and to popularize the Principality as a tourist haven (for example T.L. Llewelyn Pritchard in 'The Adventures of Twn Shon Catti') emphasized the regional differences of the clothes but they were exaggerating. One such person was Mrs Augusta Hall or Lady Llanover as she later became. About 1830 she painted a

* *Welsh Peasant Costume by F. G. Peyne.*

series of water colours of costumes she saw in Monmoutnshire and she spoke of 'national costumes'. What she meant by this was Welsh flannel and she was keen to preserve 'the national checks and stripes' of these Welsh materials. She failed to point out that there were no ancient and traditional patterns but Wales did not mind being persuaded that such patterns existed. Nevertheless, Lady Llanover was partly responsible for the birth of the dress which has been called national costume — *'it was she who turned farm servant's working clothes into a conscious, or rather self-conscious national costume.'*

To interest tourists, attractive prints of country costumes began to be produced from 1840. These suggested that Welsh women in general dressed this way and that there was 'a national costume'. Nothing is further from the truth for there is no evidence at all that Welsh women dressed in this way.

The print of the mid nineteenth century became the coloured postcard of the late nineteenth. In an effort to persuade visitors that Wales was a strange and exciting place, businessmen used women to pose in 'Welsh' costume to suggest that they were illustrations of contemporary Welsh life. 'And so,' . . . . . . by the end of the century, 'all over Wales people began to interest themselves anew in a so-called national dress that had disappeared'. The old bedgown had been exchanged for a blouse and skirt and cotton and silk were used instead of homespun and flannel. Brighter colours made the costume more fashionable, and smaller aprons were used. The bonnet worn beneath the hat was replaced by lace frills under the hat itself and frills and laces were worn at the wrists and on the bodice.

However the Welsh costume emerged, there is no doubt that it is colourful and adds to the gaiety of Eisteddfodau and Welsh gatherings today.

WELSH NOTS — Y "NOT" CYMRAEG

Hardly a custom but an imposition which is long remembered in Wales was the 19th century Welsh Nots. These were signs in wood hung as a punishment around the necks of children who spoke Welsh at school.

CAERPHILLY CHEESE — CHAWS CAERFFILI

Caerphilly Cheese originated in the Glamorganshire town of this name. It was a favourite amongst the miners who took it to work. Light and crumbly it had a texture all its own. Of late, very little Caerphilly cheese is made in its place of origin and the Caerphilly cheese market famous throughout Southern Glamorgan is a thing of the past. Devonshire and Somerset carry on the cheese-making tradition once so much alive in rural Wales.

THE KING OF BARDSEY AND THE COURT OF STRAYS —

BRENIN YNYS ENLLI A LLYS Y CRWYDRIAD

Around the coast of Wales there are a number of islands. One of these is Bardsey Island, Gwynedd. The liability of the island to be isolated in extremes of weather gave rise to a custom which is worth remembering. This is the practice of choosing an islander to decide disputes when connection with the mainland was impossible. The custom arose from an idea of one of the members of the Wynn family who owned the island and the 'crown', the 'treasure', the 'army' (denoted by a wooden effigy) and the 'king' still remain.

A similar custom still existed until recently at Dylife, Powy. There, a Court of Strays was set up by shepherds. This was held to decide the authenticity of owner-markings on the fleeces of sheep and the true parentage of lambs.

...and COOKING

COCKLES — COCOS

Cockles
Vinegar

Scrub the cockles to remove sand and grit. Place in a saucepan of salted water and boil for 3 minutes. As soon as the shells open, remove from the heat and drain. Extract the cockles from the shells with a fork. Sprinkle with vinegar on a bed of lettuce in large shells and serve with thin brown bread and butter.

COCKLE SAUCE — SAWS COCOS

2 tablespoons chopped cockles
½ oz. flour
½ oz. butter
1 teaspoon made up mustard
1 gill milk
1 gill cockle water

Extract the cockles as above and chop coarsely. Keep 1 gill of the cockle water. Melt the butter in a saucepan and stir in the flour using a wooden spoon. Stir in the milk, cockle water and mustard. Heat gently for 2-3 minutes. Add the chopped cockles and re-heat thoroughly. Serve with poached white fish and salad.

QUEEN SCALLOPS — GREGYN CYLCHOG BRENHINES

4 scallops
1 tablespoon lemon juice
2 oz. breadcrumbs
2 oz. grated cheese
½ oz. butter
salt
The sauce:
1 oz. butter
1 oz. flour
2 oz. grated cheese
½ pint milk

Scrub the scallops and place in a warm oven (325°F, 163°C, gasmark 3) until the shells open. Remove the black part and gristly fibre leaving the red coral intact. Boil in salted water with the lemon juice for 10 minutes. Drain.

To make the sauce: Melt the butter in a saucepan and stir in the flour using a wooden spoon. Stir in the milk and heat gently for 2-3 minutes. Stir in the grated cheese.

To serve: Clean the scallop shells. Place a little sauce in each shell and sprinkle with breadcrumbs. Place a scallop on top, cover with a little more sauce and sprinkle with breadcrumbs and cheese. Dot with butter and bake at the top of a fairly hot oven (375°F, 191°C gas mark 5) for 20 minutes. Garnish with parsley and serve with salad.

STEWED EELS — LLYSWENNOD WEDI'U STIWIO

2 small eels
2 small onions
4 oz. mushrooms
1 oz. butter
1 oz. flour
½ lemon
1 pint fish stock
1 tablespoon port
salt and pepper

Melt the butter in the flour and stir in the stock. Grate the lemon rind and slice the mushrooms. Skin and slice the onions, cut up the eels. Add the rind, mushrooms, onions and eels to the stock. Season to taste. Simmer gently until the fish is tender. Place the fish in the centre of a hot dish. Skim the sauce and bring back to the boil. Add the port and the pour over the eels. Serve hot.

POACHED DEE SALMON — EOG DYFRDWY MUDFERWEDIG

1 large fresh salmon
salt
1 lemon

Wash the fish in saltwater. Place whole in salted water and bring slowly to boiling point. Simmer gently allowing 10 minutes per lb. Serve cold with a mixed salad.

STUFFED SOLE — LLEDEN CHWITHIG WEDI'I STWFFIO

1 sole
1 tablespoon shrimps
2 tablespoons breadcrumbs
2 tablespoons dry white wine
1 teaspoon finely chopped parsley
½ teaspoon mixed herbs
squeeze of lemon juice
1 egg
½ pint milk
4 oz. button mushrooms
2 oz. butter
1 oz. flour
salt and pepper

Skin the sole on both sides and cut down the centre as if to fillet. Raise the fillets one inch on either side of the bone but do not remove. Mix the breadcrumbs, shrimps, parsley and herbs. Add a squeeze of lemon juice and season to taste. Lightly beat the egg and use to bind the mixture. Place this forcemeat in the fish. Put the fish in a buttered dish and pour the milk and wine around it. Bake in a moderate oven (350°, 177°C gas mark 4) for 15 minutes. Baste the fish two or three times with the liquor.

Slice the mushrooms and cook gently with 1 oz. of the butter, for 5 minutes. Remove the fish from the oven when it is cooked and drain off the liquid. Cover the fish and keep it warm. Melt remaining butter and stir in the flour using a wooden spoon. Add the stock from the fish and cook for 2-3 minutes. Drain the mushrooms on tissue paper and place on top of the fish. Cover with the sauce and serve hot.

FISH CAKES – TEISENNAU PYSGOD

½ lb. of any cooked fish
½ lb. mashed boiled potatoes
1 oz. butter
1 teaspoon chopped parsley
1 egg
breadcrumbs
salt and pepper

Remove any bones and skin from the fish and chop coarsely. Mix the fish with the potatoes, butter and parsley. Season to taste. Turn the mixture on to a floured board and form into 2 inch cakes. Whisk the egg lightly. Dip the fish cakes in the egg and then toss in the breadcrumbs. Fry in hot fat until golden brown.

OYSTERMOUTH FISH PIE – PASTAI BYSGOD YSTUMLLWYNARTH

1 lb. boiled salt cod
1 lb. mashed boiled potatoes
½ oz. butter
1 small onion
1 hard boiled egg
1 dessertspoon chopped parsley
½ teaspoon made-up mustard
1 tablespoon milk
salt and pepper.

Flake the fish and mix with the potatoes. Peel and slice the onions. Chop up the egg. Add the onion, egg and parsley to the fish mixture. Season with the mustard, pepper and salt, and mix with the milk and half of the butter. Turn into a buttered pie-dish, dot with butter and brown in a moderately hot oven (375°F, 191°C, gas mark 5). Serve hot with buttered parsnips, or with egg mayonnaise and salad.

LAVERBREAD WITH WELSH GAMMON AND EGG — BARA LAWR GYDA GAMWN CYMRU AC WYAU

Laverbread is a smooth fine seaweed found off the shores of South Wales. It is gathered daily in places like Penclawdd.

The seaweed is thoroughly washed to remove all sand and grit. It is then boiled for 5-6 hours until it is quite soft. The liquid is drained off. This prepared laverbread is sold from wooden tubs lined with white cloths in the markets of Wales. It should be used and eaten as quickly as possible.

1 lb. prepared laverbread
4 slices of Welsh gammon
2 oz. oatmeal
1 oz. baconfat
4 eggs

Fry the gammon. Melt the bacon fat in a frying pan. Divide the laverbread into 4 cakes and coat with oatmeal. Fry the laverbread in the bacon fat for 5-10 minutes. Fry the eggs in another pan. Arrange each gammon slice, laverbread cake and egg on a hot plate.

WELSH BROTH — CAWL CYMRU

2 lb. Welsh lamb
2 carrots
2 turnips
2 onions
1 oz. barley
4 pints water
1 teaspoon mixed herbs
salt and pepper

Cut the meat into pieces and remove as much fat as possible. Cover with cold water in a large saucepan. Bring to the boil and skim. Peel and slice the carrots and turnips. Skin and dice the onions. Add all the ingredients to the meat. Season to taste. Simmer for 1½-2 hours until the meat is tender. Serve hot.

FISH

The picture shows some of the fish dishes available in Wales, cockles with lemon, cockle pie, dressed crab, fresh prawn salad and fried dabs.

SOUPS

Leek and potato soup is illustrated in this picture. This makes a satisfying beginning to a dinner party but can often make a meal in itself or a first-class supper dish. As a main meal garnish with parsley and serve with new bread and salad.

MEATS

Steak and kidney pie is a traditional dish in Wales as elsewhere in the United Kingdom. It is particularly appetising served with vegetables and Gower potatoes, boiled or in their jackets.

MEATS

Crown Roast of Welsh Lamb, served with new potatoes and mixed vegetables, a sophisticated Welsh meal of today.

SWEETS

Golden sponge pudding is always a satisfying sweet. It is particularly delicious when served with syrup or a fruit sauce and cream.

CAKES

This picture illustrates Granny's Special Cake, a traditional Welsh recipe which provides an alternative to the well-known teisen lap.

PRESERVES

Home-made marmalade always tastes the best. In this picture are some of the preserves that can be made at home — orange, bitter orange, grapefruit or lemon marmalades.

DRINKS

Fruit Punch, a welcome, refreshing summer drink.

HARVEST BROTH — CAWL CYNHAEAF

2 lb. Welsh neck of lamb
½ lb. peas
½ lb. broad beans
1 small cauliflower
1 medium sized carrot
1 medium sized onion
1 medium sized turnip
2-3 lettuce leaves
5 sprigs of parsley
3 pints water
salt and pepper

Trim off as much fat as possible from the meat. Place the meat, with the water, in a large saucepan and bring to the boil. Skim carefully until the liquid is clear and as free from fat as possible. Shell the peas and beans, and peel and dice the carrot, onion and turnip. Add the vegetables to the meat and season with salt and pepper. Simmer gently for 2½ — 3 hours. Wash and clean the cauliflower and lettuce and stand in cold water for half an hour. Break the cauliflower into sprigs and finely chop the lettuce. Add to the broth half an hour before serving. Serve hot and decorate with the sprigs of parsley.

BACON SOUP – SŴP CIG MOCH

3 oz. lean bacon
1 oz. bacon fat
1 medium-sized potato
2 leeks
1 stick celery
1 egg
1 pint bacon or ham stock
¼ pint milk
2 teaspoons chopped parsely
salt and pepper

Cook and dice the bacon. Peel and slice the potato and leeks. Slice the celery. Add the vegetables to the fat and cook for a few minutes. Stir in the stock and simmer for 30 minutes. Season to taste. Separate the egg yolk from the white and blend the yolk with the milk. Remove the pan from the heat and add the milk and egg yolk. Cook for 2 – 3 minutes but do not boil. Sprinkle with parsley and serve hot.

CHICKEN AND LEEK SOUP — SWP CYW IAR A CHENNIN

1 small chicken
2 chicken stock cubes
4 pints water
6 leeks
salt and pepper

Clean and joint the chicken and add to the stock cubes dissolved in the water in a large pan. Clean leeks and remove some of the green tops. Cut into ½ inch slices and add to the stock. Season to taste and simmer for 3 hours until the meat is tender. Cool and skim off the chicken fat. Re-heat for a further 30 minutes. To serve: Remove the meat from the bones and place at the bottom of the warmed soup bowls. Pour the hot soup over the chicken.

LEEK AND POTATO SOUP – SŴP CENNIN A THATWS

3 leeks
1 lb. potatoes
2 oz. butter
1 oz. flour
3 pints chicken stock
1 cup milk
3 sprigs parsley
salt and pepper

Trim the leeks, wash thoroughly and slice finely. Peel and dice the potatoes. Place the leeks and potatoes with 1 oz. of the butter in a large saucepan. Cover with the lid and heat gently for 5 minutes until the leeks are very lightly coloured. Shake the saucepan gently to prevent the vegetables burning. Pour on the stock and simmer for ¾ hour. Melt the rest of the butter in a small saucepan and stir in the flour using a wooden spoon. Stir in the milk making sure that there are no lumps. Simmer for 2-3 minutes on a gentle heat and then add to the soup. Stir well and bring back to the boil. Serve hot garnished with parsley.

TRIPE AND ONION SOUP — SWP TREIP A WYNIWNS [NIONOD]

1 lb. tripe
1 medium sized onion
1 oz. flour
1 oz. butter
1½ pints milk and water
salt and pepper

Cut the prepared tripe into 2 inch squares. Skin and dice the onion. Season to taste. Simmer the tripe and onion in the milk and water for 1 hour until the tripe is tender. Melt the butter in another saucepan and work in the flour. Stir in a little stock from the tripe: then return this flour mixture to the main saucepan. Stir well and bring back to the boil. Cook gently for 2-3 minutes. Serve hot with boiled Gower potatoes and creamed button mushrooms.

WELSH RABBIT STEW — POTES CWNINGEN CYMRU

1 young rabbit
2 oz. butter
2 bacon rashers
2 oz. mushrooms
1 onion
1 carrot
1 potato
1 stock cube
1 tablespoon flour
1 pint water
salt and pepper

Skin and clean the rabbit. Joint the rabbit and fry in the butter. Cut up the bacon. Peel and slice the mushrooms. Skin and dice the onion. Add the bacon, mushrooms and onion to the pan. Fry lightly. Transfer the meat and vegetables from the pan to a saucepan. Work the flour into the fat in the frying pan. Dissolve the stock cube in the water and gradually stir into the flour. Bring to the boil and then pour over the meat. Peel and dice the carrot and potato and add to the soup. Season to taste. Simmer for 1 hour.

CHEESE SOUP – SWP CAWS

4 oz. cheese
1 large carrot
1 large onion
1 large potato
1 stick celery
1¼ pints water
¼ pint single cream
salt and pepper
2 teaspoons chopped parsley
2 chicken stock cubes

Peel and dice the carrot and potato. Skin and dice the onion. Cut up the celery. Dissolve the stock cubes in the water. Add the vegetables. Season to taste and simmer for 15-20 minutes until all the vegetables are soft. Grate the cheese and add with the cream. Heat but do not boil. Stir in the parsley and serve hot.

BREAST OF WELSH LAMB WITH GREEN PEAS AND MINT SAUCE — BRON OEN CYMRU GYDA PHYS FFRES A SAWS MINTYS

1 breast of Welsh lamb
1 oz. flour
1 oz. butter
1 lb. peas
1 small onion
1 pint stock
salt and pepper

Remove the skin and most of the fat from the breast. Cut the breast into pieces and dip in the flour. Skin and slice the onion. Fry the meat and onion lightly in the butter. Cover with stock, season to taste and simmer for 30 minutes. Add the peas, and simmer until the peas are tender. Place the meat in a serving dish and pour the gravy and peas over it. Serve with boiled potatoes.

MINT SAUCE — SAWS MINTYS

4 tablespoons finely chopped mint
2 tablespoons granulated sugar
1 tablespoon water
½ pint malt vinegar

Dissolve the sugar in the water. Mix all the ingredients together in a jug and stand for 30 minutes.

CROWN ROAST OF WELSH LAMB — CORON OEN CYMRU WEDI' I ROSTIO

2 best ends of neck of Welsh lamb
dripping
The stuffing
1 onion
3 oz. rice
2 oz. celery
8 oz. breadcrumbs
1 egg
1 oz. butter
salt and pepper
The gravy
1 oz. flour
liquor from the roast meat
1 pint potato water

Cook the rice in a little water. Skin and dice the onion and chop the celery finely. Lightly beat the egg. Mix all the ingredients of the stuffing together. Remove the thin bone from each joint. Cut across the bone ends of the meat, about 1½ inches from the tips. Remove the fatty ends and scrape the bones free of meat. Sew the two joints together using fine string or strong cotton and a strong needle so that the bones curve outwards forming a crown. Stand in a roasting tin and brush with melted dripping. Place the stuffing in the middle of the crown. Cover the whole with kitchen foil to keep the stuffing moist and the bones from burning. Roast in the centre of a moderate oven (350°F, 177°C, gas mark 4). Allow 30 minutes per lb. Twenty minutes from the end of cooking remove the foil, except for a small piece over the stuffing, to crisp the meat.

The gravy

Add the flour to the liquid from the meat and work in using a wooden spoon. Stir in the potato water. Boil for 2-3 minutes and add gravy browning if needed.

To serve: Decorate the bone tips with cutlet frills and serve with creamed or boiled potatoes, carrots and peas and gravy and mint sauce.

ROAST GOOSE WITH SAGE AND ONION STUFFING — GWŶDD ROST A STWFFIN SAETS A WYNIWNS

1 goose
2 oz. lard
salt and pepper

The stuffing
4 oz. onions
2 oz. breadcrumbs
1 oz. margarine
1 teaspoon sage
1 egg
salt and pepper

Clean the goose thoroughly and dry with a clean cloth or kitchen paper. Stuff the bird and close the skin with skewers. Place the goose and fat in a large tin but do not cover. Allow 15 minutes per lb and 15 minutes over. Begin in a hot oven (450°F, 232°C, gas mark 8) and after 45 minutes lower to 350°F, 177°C, gas mark 4. Then 45 minutes, and again 1¼ hours after putting the bird in the oven, and 30 minutes before serving, prick the bird all over to release fat. This makes the bird crisper. Pour away excess fat. Serve with orange sauce, peas and boiled or creamed potatoes.

The Stuffing

Peel and cut up the onions. Boil until tender in salted water. Drain and combine with the other ingredients.

MICHAELMAS GOOSE — GWŷDD GŵYL FIHANGEL

1 small goose
1 lb. onions
½ lb. oatmeal
salt and pepper

Wash and clean the goose thoroughly. Dry with a clean cloth or kitchen paper. Place in a large fish kettle and cover with cold water. When the water has boiled, turn the goose over. Boil for 2 hours, turning the goose occasionally. Remove the goose and skim as much fat as possible from the liquor. Skin and dice the onions. Make the oatmeal into a paste and stir with the onions into the soup. Boil gently until the onions are cooked and the soup thickens. Serve hot with mashed Gower potatoes and slices of goose.

POACHER'S PIE – PASTAI'R HERWHELIWR

1 young rabbit
1 lb. steak
2 small onions
½ teaspoon sage
1 oz of flour
salt and pepper
shortcrust or flaky pastry

Skin, clean and joint the rabbit. Cut up the steak. Skin and slice the onions. Place the meat, onions and sage in a saucepan of water. Season to taste. Boil until the meat is tender. Remove the rabbit bones. Place the meat in a pie dish. Thicken ½ pint of the meat stock with the flour and pour over the meat. Cover with shortcrust pastry as made on page 89 or use frozen flaky pastry. Cook in a hot oven (425°F, 218°C, gas mark 7) for 25 minutes. Serve hot with mixed vegetables.

MINCE – CIG WEDI'I FALU

1 lb. stewing steak
1 medium sized onion
½ oz. butter
2 tablespoons water or the extract
from a beef roast
salt and pepper

Remove all skin, gristle and as much fat as possible from the meat. Cut into chunks and pass through the mincer. Place in a well buttered saucepan and stir with a wooden spoon to break up any lumps. When the pink colour has disappeared, add 2 tablespoons hot water or beef extract from a beef roast. Peel and add the onion whole. Season to taste. Cover with a lid and simmer gently for 4-5 minutes, stirring occasionally. Use in a meat pie or serve with hot gravy in the centre of a platter of vegetables or on rice.

GOWER PIE – PASTAI BRO GŴYR

1 lb. mince
2 lb. Gower potatoes
1 oz. butter
1 oz. beef dripping
1 large onion
1 bouillon cube
3 tablespoons milk
1 level tablespoon flour
½ pint water
salt and pepper

Prepare the mince as on page 78 Peel and boil the potatoes. Drain off the water and cream the potatoes with the milk and butter. Skin and chop onion and fry with the dripping until the onion is soft and beginning to brown. Remove from the heat and add the flour. Dissolve the bouillon cube in the potato water, making the volume up to ½ pint with water and pour into the frying pan. Heat gently, stirring to prevent lumps forming. Add the meat, mix well and simmer for 5 minutes. Taste for seasoning. Pour the meat mixture into a buttered pie dish and cover, with the creamed potatoes. Smooth the potatoes with a knife and then mark the surface into swirls using a fork. Cook in a hot oven (425°F, 218°C, gas mark 7) for 15-20 minutes until golden brown. Serve hot with mixed vegetables.

STEAK AND KIDNEY PIE — PASTAI STEC AC AREN

12 oz. stewing steak
4 oz. ox kidney
1 tablespoon flour
½ teaspoon salt
¼ teaspoon pepper
water or stock
pastry

Mix the salt, pepper and flour. Cut the steak and kidney into small pieces and roll in the seasoned flour. Put an egg cup in the centre of a pie dish to support the pastry. Place the meat in the dish, mixing steak and kidney. Pour in water or stock to come half way up the meat. Cover with shortcrust pastry made as on page   or use frozen flaky pastry. Cut a tiny slit in the centre to allow steam to escape and make a rose for decoration from any scraps of pastry left over. Brush with a little milk. Bake in a hot oven (425°F, 218°C, gas mark 7) for 20 minutes until the pastry is brown. Then cover with a piece of greaseproof paper and lower the heat to moderate (325°F, 163°C, gas mark 3) and cook for a further 1 hour or until the meat is tender when tested with a skewer. Serve hot with boiled potatoes and vegetables.

VEAL ESCALLOPS – ESCALOPS CIG LLO

1 lb. veal
3 oz. butter
3 oz. flour
8 oz. mushrooms
½ pint water
½ pint milk
salt and pepper

Cut the veal into slices and beat gently with a rolling pin to flatten them. Sprinkle with salt and pepper and dip in flour – using 1 oz. of the flour. Melt 1 oz. of the butter in a stew pan and lightly fry the veal slices until golden brown on both sides. Add the water, and salt and pepper to taste, cover with a lid and cook gently until tender. Wash the mushrooms and cut off the base of the stalks. Skin if large. Place the mushrooms in a saucepan with the stock from the veal and simmer steadily for 6 minutes. Melt the rest of the butter in another saucepan and work in the rest of the flour. Gradually stir in the milk and bring to the boil. Add the mushrooms and liquor and cook until smooth. Check for seasoning. To serve: Pour the mushroom sauce over the meat and garnish with lemon wedges and rolls of grilled bacon or with oysters if preferred.

SNOWDONIA HOT POT — LOBSCOWS ERYRI

½ lb. skinless pork sausages
½ lb. shoulder ham
½ lb. tomatoes
1 lb. potatoes
1 apple
1 onion
1 oz. flour
1 level teaspoon mixed herbssalt and pepper
salt and pepper

Cut each sausage into three and roughly chop up the ham. Dip the meat into seasoned flour. Slice the tomatoes. Peel and slice the potatoes, apple and onion. Arrange in layers in a casserole dish, beginning with potatoes, then a layer of meat, then a mixture of apple, onion and tomato. Finish with a layer of potatoes. Season each layer lightly. Half fill the casserole with water and cook in a moderate oven (350°F, 177°C, gas mark 4) for 2 hours. Serve hot with a platter of mixed vegetables.

FAGGOTS AND PEAS — FFAGODAU A PHYS

1 lb. pig's liver
1 pig's caul
3 small onions
3 oz. breadcrumbs
1 teaspoon salt
1 teaspoon sage
½ teaspoon white pepper
½ teaspoon ground ginger
1 oz. flour
1 oz. dripping

Soak the caul in tepid water. Cut the liver into pieces. Skin and dice the onion. Simmer the liver and onion in water for ¾ hour. Drain off the liquor and keep it to make gravy. Mince the liver and onions. Mix with the breadcrumbs and add the seasoning. Mix to a smooth paste with a fork. Cut the caul into 4 inch squares. Fill each square with a ball of meat mixture and place on a greased tray. Cook in a moderate oven (350°F, 177°C, gas mark 4) for 40 minutes. Melt the dripping in a saucepan and work in the flour. Stir in the stock from the liver and onions. Bring to the boil and simmer for 2-3 minutes. Pour over the faggots and serve with green peas.

CREAM WELSH RAREBIT — HUFENGAWS WEDI POBI

4 eggs
1 oz. butter
1 oz. Cheddar cheese
1 tablespoon cream
salt and pepper

Melt the butter in a saucepan. Beat the eggs slightly and season with salt and pepper. Add the cream and pour into the saucepan. Heat gently, stirring all the time until the mixture thickens. Serve on hot buttered toast and sprinkle with grated cheddar cheese.

CAERPHILLY PUDDING — PWDIN CAERFFILI

2 oz. Caerphilly cheese
2 oz. breadcrumbs
1 oz. butter
½ pint milk
2 eggs
pinch of salt

Grate the cheese. Mix half the cheese with the breadcrumbs. Add a pinch of salt. Melt the butter in the milk and pour over the mixture. Separate the yolks and whites of the eggs. Lightly beat the yolks and stir into the cheese mixture. Bake in a moderate oven (325°F, 163°C, gas mark 3) for ½ hour. Whip the egg whites and spread over the pudding. Sprinkle with the rest of the cheese and return to the oven until brown.

CHEESE PUDDING — PWDIN CAWS

4 oz. Cheddar cheese
3 oz. bread crumbs
1 oz. butter
2 eggs
salt and pepper
½ pint milk

Heat the butter with the milk and pour over the bread crumbs. Grate the cheese. Separate the egg yolks from the whites. Beat the yolks lightly and add to the bread crumb mixture with most of the cheese. Season to taste. Whip the egg whites stiffly and fold into the mixture. Pour into a buttered pie dish and cover with the remaining cheese. Cook for 30-40 minutes in a moderate oven (350°F, 177°C, gas mark 4).

MARROW CHEESE — CAWS POMPIWN

marrow
milk
cheese
salt and pepper

Peel the marrow and cut into chunks. Remove all seeds. Boil with salted water until tender. Drain and place in a fireproof dish. Cover with grated cheese and brown under the grill.

SAVOURY OMELETTE — OMLET SAWRUS

2 eggs
1 oz. cooked ham
1 oz. butter
salt and pepper

Break the eggs into a basin and add 1 dessertspoon cold water. Season and beat lightly. Chop up the ham and add to the eggs. Heat the butter in an omelette pan and then pour in the beaten egg mixture. As the mixture sets, push it gently away from the sides of the pan and tilt so as to allow uncooked egg to reach the heat. When all the egg is just cooked, fold the omelette in half and turn on to a hot dish. Serve immediately.

SWANSEA POTATO CAKES — TEISENNAU TATWS ABERTAWE

8 oz. Gower boiled potatoes
2 oz. flour
½ oz. butter
1 egg
4 rashers of Welsh bacon

Mash the potatoes with the butter. When cool, add the egg, lightly beaten. Add enough of the flour to make a consistency that is firm enough to handle. Form the mixture into flat 2 inch cakes. Fry 4 slices of Welsh bacon and then fry the potato cakes in the bacon fat. Serve the potato cakes and bacon alone or with egg and laverbread.

TOMATO CHEESE — CAWS TOMATO

8 oz. tomatoes
2 oz. grated Cheddar cheese
2 oz. breadcrumbs
1 oz. butter
1 small onion
1 egg

Dip the tomatoes in boiling water for a few minutes to loosen the skins. Remove the skins and cook the tomatoes with the butter until soft. Skin and dice the onion and simmer with a little water until soft. Drain and add with the other ingredients to the tomatoes. Stir until the cheese dissolves. Cool. Use to spread on rolls and decorate with thin slices of cucumber.

MARROW CHUTNEY — SHWTNI POMPIWN

2½ lb. marrow
1oz. salt
4 oz. onions
4 oz. raisins
4 oz. sultanas
4 oz. currants
4 oz. brown sugar
½ oz. ground ginger
1 oz. mustard seed
½ pint vinegar

Peel the marrow, remove the seeds and cut the soft flesh into cubes. Sprinkle with salt and leave to stand for 24 hours. Skin and dice the onions. Simmer gently in water until they are tender. Stone the raisins. Wash and dry the fruit. Drain and wash the marrow. Add all the ingredients to the pan and simmer for 2 hours until the mixture is thick. Pour into 3 hot sterilized 1 lb. jars. Seal and leave for 2 months before serving.

LANDRINDOD WELLS PUDDING — PWDIN LLANDRINDOD

3 eggs
the weight of the eggs in their shells
of self-raising flour,
butter and castor sugar
a squeeze of lemon juice

The sauce
1 tablespoon cornflour
1 oz. sugar
½ oz. butter
½ pint milk
1 tablespoon sherry

Put the eggs, flour, butter and castor sugar in a basin and beat lightly, until well mixed. Add a squeeze of lemon juice. Pour into a buttered basin and cover with buttered greaseproof paper. Steam for 4 hours. Serve with sherry sauce.

Blend the cornflour and a little of the cold milk. Heat the rest of the milk and when just boiling pour over the cornflour, stirring all the time. Return to the saucepan with the sugar, and cook for 2-3 minutes until the sauce is thick and smooth. Add the butter and stir. Remove from the heat and add the sherry. Pour over the pudding when serving.

HARVEST CAKE — TEISEN GYNHAEF

Shortcrust pastry
8 oz. plain flour
4 oz. butter or margarine
8 teaspoons cold water
pinch salt

The filling
fruit in season
castor sugar

The pastry. Sift the flour and salt together. Rub in the fat until the mixture looks like breadcrumbs. Add the water and make into a large lump using a knife. Roll out half the pastry and line a deep ovenproof dinner plate. Clean and prepare the fruit. Cover the pastry with fruit. Add 1 tablespoon water and castor sugar to taste. Roll out the remaining pastry and cover the fruit. Brush the top with a little milk and sprinkle lightly with sugar. Bake in the centre of a fairly hot oven (425°F, 218°C, gas mark 7) for 20 minutes. Reduce the temperature (375°F, 191°C, gas mark 5) and cook for a further 20 minutes. Serve hot or cold with cream.

BAKEWELL PUDDING — PASTAI 'BAKEWELL'

Shortcrust pastry
4 oz. breadcrumbs
4 oz. castor sugar
4 oz. butter
2 dessertspoons raspberry jam
3 eggs
1 lemon

Make the shortcrust pastry as on page 89 using half the quantities. Line a fireproof dish with the pastry and spread the jam over it: Grate the rind of the lemon. Cream the butter. Mix the butter, lemon juice, rind, sugar and bread crumbs. Lightly beat the eggs and add to the mixture. Spread the mixture over the jam and bake in a fairly hot oven (400°F, 204°C, gas mark 6) for 25 minutes. Serve hot with fresh cream or custard.

GOLDEN SPONGE PUDDING — PASTAI SBWNG TRIAGL MELYN

4 oz. flour
2 oz. butter
½ oz. ground ginger
½ teaspoon baking powder
2 tablespoons milk
2 tablespoons golden syrup
1 egg

Cream the butter and lightly beat the egg. Mix all the ingredients together, pour into a buttered dish and steam for 1 hour. Serve hot with whipped cream or syrup.

90

RAISIN PIE — PASTAI RHESIN

Shortcrust pastry
8 oz. seedless, washed raisins
1 tablespoon golden syrup
1 tablespoon Demerara sugar
2 tablespoons rum
1 small orange
¼ pint cream

Prepare the shortcrust pastry as on page 89 . Roll out two-thirds of the pastry and line a 7in. flan tin. Wash the orange and grate the rind, removing all pith first. Mix the rasins, golden syrup, orange juice and grated orange rind together. Add 1 tablespoon rum. Spread the fruit mixture over the pastry in the flan tin. Roll out the remaining pastry and cut into ¼ inch wide strips. Use to criss-cross the fruit. Sprinkle with Demerara sugar. Bake in the centre of a hot oven (425°F, 218°C, gas mark 7) for 25 minutes until the pastry is cooked. When the pie is cold, lightly whip the cream and remaining rum. Drop teaspoonfuls of the cream into alternate lattice squares.

SOURCREAM TART — TARTEN HUFEN SUR

4 oz. plain flour
2 oz. butter
2 dessertspoons cold water
a pinch of salt
the filling
½ pint cream
1 oz. castor sugar
1 oz. sultanas

Sift the flour and salt together — rub in the fat until the mixture looks like breadcrumbs. Stir in the water using a knife and form into a ball. Roll out on a well floured board. Line a flan tin with the pastry. Place a circle of greaseproof paper over the pastry and keep in place with crusts of bread or haricot beans. Cook for 15 minutes in a fairly hot oven (400°F, 204°C or gas mark 6). Remove the paper and bread or beans. Sprinkle the pastry with the castor sugar and sultanas. Add the cream and return to the oven for a further 10 minutes.

GRAN'S SPECIAL CAKE — TEISEN ARBENNIG MAMGU (NAIN)

12 oz. flour
8 oz. sugar
4 oz. butter
8 oz. sultanas
2 eggs
1 teaspoon ground cloves
1 teaspoon ground caraways
1 teaspoon ground cinnamon
½ teaspoon bicarbonate of soda

Rub the butter into the flour until the mixture is like breadcrumbs. Stir in the sugar, sultanas and spices. Beat the eggs lightly. Dissolve the bicarbonate of soda in a teaspoon of water and add with the eggs. Mix well using a metal spoon. Turn into a buttered 8 inch cake tin and place in a hot oven (425°F, 218°C, gas mark 7). After 15-20 minutes or when the cake is well risen, lower the heat (375°F, 191°C, gas mark 5) and cook for a further 1¼ hours.

PANCAKE DELIGHT — CREMPOG (FFROIS) MELYS

4 oz. flour
1 egg
½ pint milk and water
pinch of salt
lard for frying
sugar and lemon juice
1 small can sliced peaches
½ pint whipped cream

Sift the flour and salt together. Make a hole in the centre of the flour and add the egg. Add 2 tablespoons of liquid and stir until all the ingredients are mixed well together. Add half the remaining liquid and beat until the batter is smooth. Stir in the rest of the liquid. Heat a little lard in a frying pan until it begins to 'haze'. Pour just enough batter into the pan to cover the bottom. Fry, using a moderate heat, shaking the pan gently so that the pancake does not stick to the pan. Turn and cook the other side. Turn on to a warm plate and sprinkle with sugar and lemon juice. Drain the peaches and place 2 or 3 slices in the centre of the pancake. Roll-up. Close the ends with stars of whipped cream. Serve immediately.

OATCAKES — CACENNAU CEIRCH

4 oz. oatmeal
1 teaspoon dripping
a pinch of bicarbonate of soda
a pinch of salt
hot water

Mix the dry ingredients together in a bowl. Melt the fat. Stir the fat and a little hot water into the mixture to make a stiff paste. Turn on to a board dusted with oatmeal and roll out thinly. Cut into 6 wedges and cook on a moderately hot griddle or thick frying pan until the edges begin to curl. Turn and cook the other side until golden brown. Serve buttered with honey, or marmalade, cheese or sardines.

GRIDDLE SCONES — BARA'R RADELL [BARA PLANC]

4 oz. flour
1 oz. sugar
1 oz. sultanas
2 teaspoons baking powder
1 egg
¼ pint milk
pinch of salt

Sift the flour, sugar, baking powder and salt into a basin. Add the fruit. Lightly beat the egg and stir into the mixture. Add enough milk to make a batter with a consistency of thick cream. Grease and warm the griddle, electric hot plate or thick frying pan. The temperature is right when a teaspoon of the batter mixtures goes golden brown within 1 minute of being dropped on the griddle. Keep the heat constant. Drop spoonfuls of the batter on the griddle. Cook for two minutes, turn and cook for a further two minutes. The scones should feel firm. Cool on a wire tray.

94

WELSH CAKES — PICAU AR Y MAEN

8 oz. flour
4 oz. butter
3 oz. castor sugar
2 oz. currants
1 teaspoon baking powder
¼ teaspoon mixed spice
2 tablespoons milk
pinch of salt
1 egg

Sift the flour, baking powder, spice and salt together. Rub in the butter until the mixture looks like breadcrumbs. Add the sugar and fruit. Beat the egg. Add with enough milk to make a firm paste. Roll out on a floured board to a thickness of ¼ inch and cut into 2 inch rounds. Grease a griddle or electric hot plate or thick frying pan. Cook the cakes on the griddle over a gentle heat for three minutes on each side or until golden brown. Cool and sprinkle with castor sugar. Serve alone or with butter.

WHOLEMEAL SCONES — SCONAU GWENITH

6 oz. wholemeal
6 oz. flour
3 oz. butter
1 dessertspoon treacle
2 teaspoons baking powder
½ teaspoon salt
milk to mix

Mix the wholemeal, flour, salt and baking powder. Rub in the butter until the mixture looks like breadcrumbs. Stir in the treacle and enough milk to make a soft dough. Rollout gently on a floured board to a thickness of $\frac{1}{4}$ inch. Cut into 2 inch rounds and cook on a floured baking tin near the top of a hot oven (425°F, 218°C gas mark 7) for ten minutes. Cool on a tray. To serve, cut in half and butter.

STRAWBERRY SWEET — MEFUS MELYS

1½ lb. strawberries
1½ lb. red currants
1½ lb. castor sugar
cream

Hull and wash the strawberries and spread them on a large plate or tray (not metal). Sprinkle them with half the sugar, making sure that all the berries are sugared. Cover lightly with a sheet of greasproof paper and leave to stand overnight in a cool place. When the strawberries are ready, wash the red currants and strain the juice from them. Make up to 1 pint with water and boil with the rest of the sugar. Simmer the strawberries in this syrup until they are jellied. Pour into individual glasses. Serve cold, decorated with whipped cream and topped by a strawberry.

APPLE ALMONDS – ALMONNAU AFAL

4 small cooking apples
8 oz. granulated sugar
1 oz. blanched almonds
2 tablespoons bramble or
red currant jelly
1 pint water

The apples should be firm. Dissolve the sugar in the water. Core the apples and boil gently in this syrup. When they are cooked, but not broken, remove the apples and place on a serving dish. Boil the syrup rapidly for a few minutes to reduce it. Stick slices of blanched almonds into the apples and fill the centres with jelly. When cold, pour the syrup over the apples. Serve with custard or whipped cream.

APPLE FRITTERS – CREMPOG AFALAU

2 cooking apples
4 oz. flour
½ teaspoon salt
1 dessertspoon castor sugar
1 dessertspoon brandy
1 egg
¼ pint milk and water
lard for frying

Sift the flour, sugar and salt together. Break the egg into the middle of the flour. Add a little of the milk and water and gradually mix in the flour. Add the rest of the liquid slowly, beating until smooth. Stir in the brandy. Peel and core the apples. Cut into rings. Heat the lard until it is hot enough to brown a cube of bread in 1 minute. Dip an apple ring in the batter and then place in the fat. Cook 2 or 3 rings at a time until they are golden brown. Turn once. Drain on kitchen paper. Dust with castor sugar and serve with whipped cream.

COTTAGE LOAF — TORTH FWTHYN

3 lb. plain flour
1 oz. salt
3 tablespoons oil or
margarine
1 tablespoon dried yeast
1 teaspoon sugar
1½ pints warm water

Sieve the flour and salt together into a large bowl. Dissolve the sugar in the water and sprinkle the yeast on top. Leave to stand for 10-15 minutes until the mixture is frothy. Make a well in the middle of the flour. Add the yeast liquid and oil. Work to a firm dough which leaves the bowl cleanly. Turn on to a floured board and knead lightly until the dough is no longer sticky and a slight dent made with the finger tip comes out. Cover with a cloth and leave in a warm place for 1-1½ hours until the dough has risen to twice its original size. Knead again until firm. Divide the mixture into four to make 4 loaves. Divide each piece of dough into two and form 2 rounds, one bigger than the other. Moisten and place the smaller round one on top of the larger one on a greased and floured baking tin. Leave to rise for a further 15-20 minutes. Cook in a very hot oven (450°F, 232°C gas mark 8) for 30-40 minutes until the bread sounds hollow when tapped. Leave to cool on a wire rack.

BROWN BREAD — BARA BROWN

1½ lb. plain white flour
1½ lb. wholemeal flour
1 oz. salt
3 tablespoons oil or margarine
1 tablespoon dried yeast
1 teaspoon sugar
1½ pints warm water

Make as for cottage loaf on page 98 Divide into four and place in 4 greased and floured 1 lb. bread tins. Cover and leave to rise in a warm place for a further 15-20 minutes until the dough fills the tins. Bake in a very hot oven (450°F, 232°C, gas mark 8) for 30-35 minutes until the bread sounds hollow when tapped. Turn out and cool on a wire rack.

WHOLEMEAL BREAD — BARA GWENITH

Make and bake as for brown bread above but use stone ground or wholemeal flour. Use a little more liquid so that the dough is soft and beat with a wooden spoon instead of kneading it.

BUTTERMILK BREAD — BARA LLAETH ENWYN

1 lb. flour
1 oz. sugar
1 oz. butter
1 teaspoon bicarbonate of soda
1 teaspoon cream of tartar
pinch of salt
½ pint buttermilk or thick sour milk

Sift the flour, sugar, bicarbonate of soda, cream of tartar and salt into a bowl. Rub in the butter. Make a well in the middle of the flour mixture and add the buttermilk. Work into a firm dough. Place in a floured bread-tin and brush the top with a little milk. Bake in a moderate oven (350°F, 177°C, gas mark 4) for 45 minutes or until the bread is risen and firm.

MONEY BREAD — BARA MÊL

8 oz. flour
2 oz. butter
1 oz. sugar
2 tablespoons honey
2 tablespoons milk
1 teaspoon baking powder
¼ teaspoon salt
½ teaspoon mixed spice
1 egg

Cream the butter and sugar until light and fluffy. Beat in the honey. Whisk the egg and milk together. Sieve the flour, baking powder, salt and spice together and add with the egg and milk. Place in a greased tin and bake in a moderate oven (375°F, 191°C gas mark 5) for 40-45 minutes.

CHUNKY LEMON MARMALADE — MARMALED LEMWYN TALPIOG

2 lb. lemons
4 lb. preserving sugar
4 pints water

Wipe the fruit clean and peel. Remove the pith and cut up the peel into chunks. Cut up the fruit and collect the pips. Grease a large saucepan and add the water, fruit and peel. Tie the pips and pith in a muslin bag and add to the fruit mixture. Bring to the boil and simmer for 1½ hours until the skin is tender. Remove the muslin bag and when cooled, squeeze any juice in it back into the pan. Add the sugar and heat gently, stirring, until the sugar dissolves. Then boil rapidly, without stirring, for 35-40 minutes until the marmalade reaches the setting point. That is the temperature, using a sugar thermometer is 200°F-220°F or a little of the fruit mixture when dropped on a cold plate forms a firm wrinkled drop. Test for the setting point after 25-30 minutes so that the mixture is not over-cooked and spoiled. Allow to cool, skim and stir before putting in warm, sterilized jars. Cover with a waxed disc.

RASPBERRY JAM – JAM MAFON

1 lb. raspberries
1¼ lb. preserving sugar

Wash and clean the fruit. Heat the raspberries without any liquid to extract the juice and pectin. Add the sugar, heat gently and stir until the sugar has dissolved. Then boil rapidly until the setting point is reached in about 3 minutes for garden fresh raspberries, in about 10 minutes for shop fruit. Bottle in warm, sterilized jars and cover with a waxed disc.

BLACKBERRY AND APPLE JAM – JAM MWYAR DUON AC AFAL

1 lb. apples (after peeling
and coring)
1 lb. blackberries
2 lb. sugar
2 tablespoons water

Slice the apples and simmer gently in the water until soft. Wwash the blackberries, add to the apples and heat gently until the fruit is soft. Stir in the sugar. Continue to heat gently and stir until the sugar is dissolved. Then boil rapidly until the setting point is reached as in the preparation of marmalade on page 101. Pot in warm sterilized jars and cover with waxed discs.

LEMON CHEESE — CAWS LEMWN

8 oz. castor sugar
5 oz. butter
2 eggs
2 lemons

Peel the lemons as thinly as possible. Remove any pith from the rind and grate the rind. Place the rind, lemon juice, sugar and butter in a double saucepan or in a basin standing in a saucepan half full of boiling water. Stir to blend the ingredients. Lightly beat the eggs and stir the lemon mixture into them. Strain the mixture into the double saucepan or basin and continue heating slowly until the mixture comes to the boil and is thick and creamy.

WALNUT FUDGE — TAFFI MEDDAL CNAU FFRENGIG

1 lb. brown sugar
4 oz. walnuts
½ pint single cream
1 tablespoon golden syrup
½ teaspoon vanilla essence

Stir the sugar, cream and syrup in a saucepan over a gentle heat. Boil for 15-20 minutes. Remove from the heat, stir in the vanilla and walnuts. Stand the saucepan in a bowl of cold water. Stir the fudge until it thickens. Pour into a buttered tin and leave to set. When nearly set, cut into squares.

CARDIGAN TOFFEE — TAFFI CEREDIGION

12 oz. granulated sugar
1 oz. ground almonds
½ oz. butter
6 tablespoons milk

Butter a tin measuring 6 inch by 4 inch and 1 inch deep. Melt the butter in a thick saucepan or double saucepan over a low heat. Add the sugar, almonds, butter and milk and stir well. Boil gently for seven minutes, stirring all the time. Scrape off any solid formed on the sides of the saucepan and return to the mixture. Remove from the heat and continue to stir until the toffee thickens. Pour into the tin and leave in a cool place to set. Break into pieces.

TREACLE TOFFEE — TAFFI TRIAGL [LOSIN DU]

8 oz. Demerara sugar
4 oz. black treacle
4 oz. golden syrup
1½ oz. butter
pinch of cream of tartar
teaspoon vinegar

Butter a tin measuring 6 inch by 4 inch and 1 inch deep. Heat the butter, sugar, treacle, syrup and cream of tartar in a heavy based saucepan, or better, a double saucepan, over a low heat. Stir until all the sugar has dissolved. Bring to the boil, and add the vinegar. Continue heating, without stirring, until the brittle point is reached, i.e., a sugar thermometer registers 270°F or a few drops of the toffee mixture become brittle when poured into a cup of cold water. Pour into the tin and leave in a cool place to set. Break into pieces.

LEMONADE — LEMONED

1 lemon
½ teaspoon bicarbonate
of soda
½ pint water
sugar

Squeeze the lemon juice into the water and add sugar to taste. Add the bicarbonate of soda, stir and serve immediately.

ORANGEADE — ORENED

6 oranges
6 oz sugar
2 pints water

Peel two of the oranges, removing as much pith as possible. Add the peel with the sugar to ½ pint of water and simmer gently for 20 minutes. Squeeze the juice from all the oranges into a jug and add the remaining water. When cool, strain and add the orange syrup. Serve with crushed ice.

FRUIT PUNCH — PWNS FFRWYTHAU

1 lb. mixed fruits —
strawberries, raspberries
grapes, oranges, apples
1 pint unsweetened apple juice
1 pint orange juice
1 pint ginger ale

Wash the fruit, peel and slice if necessary. Put the fruit into a large bowl and add the liquid. Stir. Serve in tall glasses with ice.

MULLED CLARET — CLARED MELYSDWYM

1 bottle sherry or claret
1 pint boiling water
1 tablespoon castor sugar
4 tablespoons brandy
powdered cinnamon
1 lemon

Warm (but do not boil) a bottle of sherry or claret. Slice the lemon and place in a warmed jug. Pour the hot wine over the fruit and then add the hot water, sugar and brandy. Serve hot, dusted with cinnamon.

WINE FRUIT CUP — CWPAN GWIN FFRWYTHAU

1 bottle sauterne
1 bottle soda water
4 oz. sugar
8 oz. strawberries
3 oranges
1 pineapple

Cut up the oranges and pineapple into chunks. Add the strawberries. Dissolve the sugar in a cup of water and pour over the fruit. When cold, put in a punch bowl with plenty of ice. Pour in the sauterne and soda water. Stir.

APRICOT BRANDY — BRANDI BRICYLLEN

12 apricots
½ lb. sugar
1 pint brandy

Cut up the apricots into small pieces. Crush the kernels and add to the fruit. Place in a screw top jar with the sugar. Cover with 1 pint of brandy. Close the jar tightly and leave to stand for 1 month. Shake occasionally. Strain and re-bottle.

CUSTOMS — INDEX

RECIPES — INDEX

Cakes and Sweets
Apple almonds, 97
Apple fritters, 97
Bakewell pudding, 90
Golden sponge pudding, 90
Gran's special cakes, 92
Griddle cakes, 94
Harvest cake, 89
Llandrindod Wells pudding, 88
Oat cakes, 94
Pancake delight, 93
Raisin pie, 91
Sour cream tart, 92
Strawberry sweet, 96
Welsh cakes, 95
Wholemeal scones, 95

Bread
Brown bread, 99
Buttermilk bread, 100
Cottage loaf, 98
Honey bread, 100
Wholemeal bread, 99

Jams and Confectionery
Blackberry and apple jam, 102
Cardigan toffee, 104
Chunky lemon marmalade, 101
Lemon cheese, 103
Raspberry jam, 102
Treacle toffee, 104
Walnut fudge, 103

Wines and Beverages
Apricot brandy, 107
Fruit punch, 106
Lemonade, 105
Milled claret, 106
Orangeade, 105
Wine fruit cup, 107

COOKING TEMPERATURES

Oven Description	Electric Oven Setting	Gas Oven Setting
Very cool	250° F. (121° C.)	$\frac{1}{4}$
	275° F. (135° C.)	$\frac{1}{2}$
Cool	300° F. (149° C.)	1, 2
Warm	325° F. (163° C.)	3
Moderate	350° F. (177° C.)	4
Fairly hot	375° F. (191° C.)	5
	400° F. (204° C.)	6
Hot	425° F. (218° C.)	7
Very hot	450° F. (232° C.)	8
	500° F. (240° C.)	9

WEIGHTS AND MEASURES

1 oz. (approx.)	Level Tablespoonsful
Breadcrumbs	3
Cheese grated	3
Cocoa	3
Butter or margarine	2
Flour .. :.	3
Oatmeal	$2\frac{1}{2}$
Rice	2
Sugar, granulated	2
Treacle	$1\frac{1}{2}$
Sultanas, currants	2
Salt	$1\frac{3}{4}$

Water freezes at 32° F. (0° C.)
Water boils at 212° F. (100° C.)
$x°$ F. $= \frac{5}{9}(x\text{-}32)°$ C.
$x°$ C. $= \left[(x \times \frac{9}{5}) + 32\right]°$ F.

Metric/Avoirdupois Weights
1 gram = 0.035 oz.
100 gram = $3\frac{1}{2}$ oz.
250 gram = 9 oz.
1 kilogram = $2\frac{1}{4}$ lb.

Avoirdupois/Metric Weights
1 oz. = 28.35 grams
4 oz. = 113.4 grams
1 lb. = 453.6 grams

ACKNOWLEDGEMENTS

No one who writes on Welsh cooking can be unaware of the excellent articles on this subject in 'South Wales Magazine'. To Bobby Freeman and others who have given me a real interest in Welsh cooking I must express my thanks.

The writers on Welsh custom in English and the vernacular are legion but I must express my gratitude to those, especially in the Welsh Museum and library services, who have helped in my researches into this subject.

I must also express my thanks to Mr Degwel Owen, Head of the Department of Welsh at the Swansea College of Education, for the Welsh translations.

Finally, I wish to record my appreciation to the following for permission to use photographs:-

Colour Library International
Picturepoint
Syndication International

Printed and published in Wales by Celtic Educational (Services) Ltd., Swansea SA1 6EA U.K.